# Stansted
# Norman Foster
# and the architecture
# of flight

A Blueprint Monograph
Published by Fourth Estate/Wordsearch

By Kenneth Powell

With photographs by
Richard Bryant and Philip Sayer

# Stansted
# Norman Foster
# and the architecture
# of flight

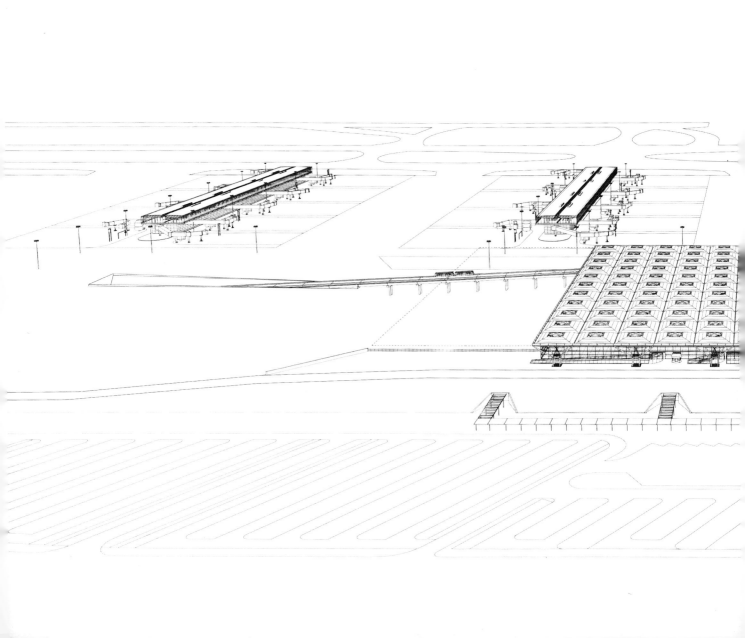

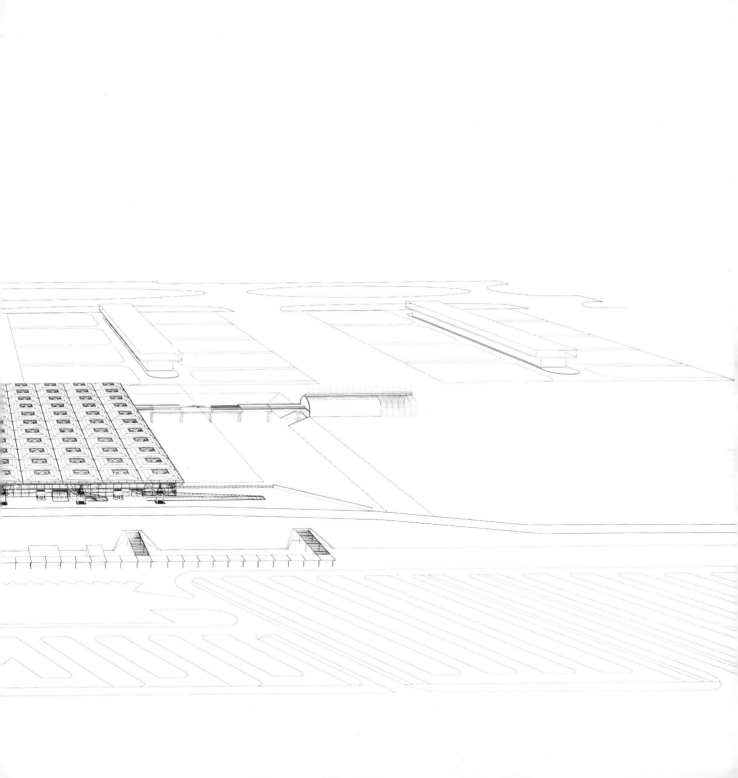

First published in Great Britain in 1992
by Fourth Estate Ltd, 289 Westbourne
Grove, London W11 2QA in conjunction
with *Blueprint* magazine, 26 Cramer
Street, London W1M 3HE

Copyright © 1992 Kenneth Powell
Fourth Estate and Wordsearch Ltd

A catalogue record for this book is
available from the British Library.

ISBN 1-872-180-99X

**Design** Esterson Lackersteen
**Series editor** Arthur Valenzuela
**Page makeup** Spy Graphics
**Colour reproduction**
Fotographics Ltd. UK/Hong Kong
**Printed and bound in Hong Kong**

**Acknowledgements**
I should like to thank the following
for their generous help with the
preparation of this book: Sir Norman
Foster, Katy Harris, Eric Lomas, Martin
Manning, Sir Norman Payne, Jane
Priestman, and above all, Spencer
de Grey, Foster Associates' Senior
Director at Stansted, who was
my guide throughout.

**Photographic credits**
Richard Bryant/Arcaid front cover,
10/11, 12/13, 73, 76/77, 78, 79, 80, 81,
82/83, 84, 85, 87; Richard Davies 30, 36,
38, 39, 42/43, 44, 47; Norman Foster 31;
Andrew Holligan 48, 88; Ken Kirkwood
2/3, 6/7, 74/75, 86; Philip Sayer 16, 24,
50, 53, 55, 56/57, 59, 60, 62, 65, 67, 68

**Blueprint Monographs**
*Ron Arad: Restless Furniture*
Deyan Sudjic
*Nigel Coates: The City in Motion*
Rick Poynor
*Rei Kawakubo and Comme des Garçons*
Deyan Sudjic
*Eva Jiricna: Design in Exile*
Martin Pawley
*King and Miranda:*
*The Poetry of the Machine*
Hugh Aldersey-Williams
*Javier Mariscal:*
*Designing the New Spain*
Emma Dent Coad
*Queensberry Hunt:*
*Creativity and Industry*
Susannah Walker
*Rodney Kinsman:*
*The Logical Art of Furniture*
Jose Manser
*Stansted: Norman Foster and*
*the Architecture of Flight*
Kenneth Powell
*Rick Mather*
Hugh Pearman

# Chapter one

# A new sort of airport

The terminal building at "Stansted Airport, London" twenty-five years ago was a model of uncompromising, severely functional, coolly anonymous modern design. It consisted of a Nissen hut – a structure conceived during the First World War to shelter troops.

Nineteen sixty-six was the year that the British Airports Authority, as it then was, took over control of Stansted. BAA plc, as it has now become, recently celebrated the silver jubilee of its association with Stansted by opening a new £108 million plus terminal building, described by its architect Sir Norman Foster as "elegantly anonymous", which brings Stansted from relative obscurity into the forefront of international airport design and ranks among the first of a new generation of major public buildings in late twentieth-century Britain.

The very term "Stansted Airport, London" was a piece of bravado in 1966. Stansted had yet to be formally designated as London's third airport, and a Government inquiry into the matter had been plodding on for several years. In summer, 1967, a White Paper was issued which shocked rural Essex to the bones. The new airport, it proposed, should be at Stansted, a few miles from the market town of Bishop's Stortford.

BAA pressed on with a more permanent, if still comparatively modest, terminal building at Stansted (completed in 1969), but protests against developing the site were strident and could not be ignored. A further inquiry, chaired by Lord Roskill, recommended a new airport in Buckinghamshire, but a strong lobby grew for the "offshore solution": the development of reclaimed land in the Thames Estuary to the east of London. Then in 1971, Edward Heath's Conservative government – conscious, no doubt, of the strength of feeling in the Tory shires – took the easy way out and declared that the new airport was to be at Maplin Sands, off the Essex coast. Stansted was to be allowed to tick along as a small regional airport, the shires went back to sleep, and nothing further was done to implement the Maplin plan.

The people of Essex had in fact got used to hearing the noise of aircraft engines during the Second World War. The main runway – over a mile long – was laid down in 1943 for the Flying Fortresses of the US Air Force's 344 Medium Bombardment Group. By 1946, after a year or so of occupation by the Royal Air Force, a new era seemed to have begun when civil flights started using Stansted regularly. Within a few years the Americans were also back in force: the Cold War had begun. A new, far longer,

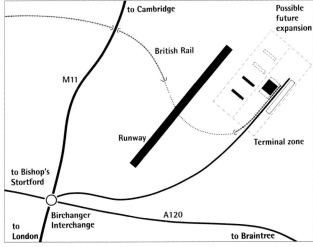

to Cambridge

British Rail

Possible future expansion

M11

Runway

Terminal zone

to Bishop's Stortford

to London

Birchanger Interchange

A120

to Braintree

**Stansted airport is approximately 32 miles north of central London and 14 miles north of the M25 orbital motorway. The M11 passes immediately to the west of the airport, providing good access from London, the M25, Cambridge and the North. The construction of a spur from the existing London-to-Cambridge rail line connects the new terminal with Liverpool Street Station**

runway was laid down to serve B47 jet bombers, at that time the West's most formidable warplanes. Stansted looked set to become the Greenham Common of the 1950s. But the military revival was brief – the USAF moved deeper into East Anglia.

Stansted soon reverted to a mixture of civil and RAF Transport Command use. Despite the Maplin decision (who even remembers it today?), Stansted remained the obvious place for a new international airport. Nevertheless, the slow rise of Gatwick (where the first large-scale terminal was opened in 1958) and the expansion of Heathrow allowed successive governments to duck the issue of a third London airport. In the mid-1970s, however, attention shifted from the Maplin project, and the government asked BAA to come forward with a plan to develop Stansted.

BAA's former chairman, and Sir John Egan's predecessor, was Sir Norman Payne. An engineer by training, Payne joined the organisation in 1965 as Engineering Director, became Chief Executive in 1972 and Chairman five years later, and saw BAA through the period of privatisation. It was Sir Norman who inherited the challenge of building the new Stansted. It was a fate, one senses, that he relished.

The key to the terminal layout was the desire of Foster Associates to return to the simplicity and convenience of the early days of flying. All public areas are on a single concourse floor – the passenger arrives at one side of the building and progresses directly through to the other side, always at the same level

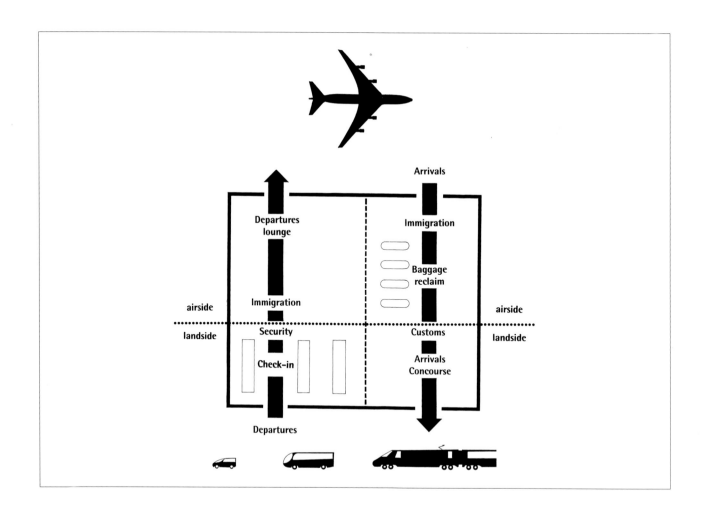

Norman Payne affects abrasive scepticism where aesthetics are concerned. Architects, he says, are facilitators: "the passengers pay, not the architects. Architects don't have to actually deal with the public at all. Our customers care above all about efficiency and cleanliness, not architectural details." But he has firm opinions as to which airports function well and look good: Newark ("underrated"), Chicago's O'Hare ("... but difficult to clean"), the recent extensions at Los Angeles, Cincinnatti, Singapore, Frankfurt and Paris's Charles de Gaulle do not, on the other hand, inspire his admiration. The alliance of the two Normans was to be a potent one.

The momentous election year of 1979 marked the beginning of Stansted's recent history. Government research had confirmed BAA's view that a third airport was still a necessity. The 1970s energy scare was over and air travel was again booming. There was also growing concern about London's place in a new Europe. If London's airports became intolerably congested, would long-haul travellers switch to Paris, Amsterdam and Frankfurt instead? As France laid down her TGV express rail network and the prospect of a Channel Tunnel moved from fantasy to possibility, this prospect became seriously worrying. The pressure was on again to site the new airport in Essex.

Norman Foster likes to show a pair of slides which illustrate the impact of his new terminal on the landscape. One is a photomontage, made early on in the design process. The other shows the completed building (which stands on a rise in the land) from the same viewpoint, a mile away. The two views are, of course, all but identical. Stansted is, says Foster, "rooted in the ecology of the area". It is a "green" building, he argues, "but not in a hair-shirt way – it's a celebratory structure."

Late in 1979 it became clear that BAA had broad Government support for its renewed plans to develop Stansted. Nonetheless, a full-scale public inquiry was set up, what Norman Foster considered just another instance of the sort of bureaucratic delays which obstruct many serious building projects in the UK. Only in June 1985, did the Government announce that it would approve BAA's planning application. After two decades of talk, London was to get its third airport. Initially, however, Stansted was only given approval to develop for half the number of the passengers originally envisaged by BAA. A further phase would have to go back for parliamentary approval.

"We'd known for years", says Norman Payne, "that the ideal airport terminal was a large open space on one level – like the Olympia exhibition hall, say. The advantages were clear, but the bitter fact is that one-level terminals need a lot of space." At Stansted, he explains, in contrast to Heathrow and even Gatwick, that space existed. It was the ideal place to build the one-level terminal of the future.

Fresh from the Hong Kong Bank, Spencer de Grey became Foster Associates' project director at Stansted. His version of events differs somewhat from that of Norman Payne's. The various options that the architects were initially given by BAA were all, he insists, based on the idea of a multi-level terminal. "The architects", says de Grey, "fought for the one-level format." Norman Foster is even more adamant. "From the very beginning", Foster says, "we felt that a single level was the only way. We sold the idea to BAA." Yet the acceptance of the idea by the clients, the architects say, suggests that Norman Payne saw its logic and had independently come to the conclusion that a one-level building was the right course at Stansted.

The idea of a single level was hardly new, although the implications, especially for servicing, had not been fully worked out. YRM, overall architects at Gatwick since the mid-fifties, had considered this possibility for the North Terminal (begun 1983), but quickly ruled it out in favour of a three-storey building because of the constricted site.

Foster Associates' brief was rooted in BAA's stated objectives: a more convenient, safer terminal for travellers; adaptability; the possibility of phased construction (an objective which subsequently became a vital condition); the ability to accommodate the largest aircraft of the foreseeable future – up to 800 seats; and lastly economy. This final requirement reflected the high cost of BAA's recent projects: proportionally, Stansted had to be at least 10 per cent cheaper. Norman Payne never seems to have doubted that Foster Associates were ideally qualified to meet the formula of economy and innovation. Together client and architect planned a unique monument.

If the needs of the travelling public rated high in the design brief, the requirements of the airlines could hardly be a secondary consideration. Some favoured the detached "unit" terminals familiar from New York's JFK and Paris's Charles de Gaulle airports. Another approach, more familiar in Britain, would have been the construction of piers radiating from the main terminal and leading to gates. But it is this arrangement which leads to the lengthy treks through passages and corridors typical of Heathrow. It was rejected, as was the idea of mobile lounges, which held some appeal to Foster (lounge-to-airport in one easy move). The rapid transit option, used at Gatwick for the first time outside the USA, was chosen (and subsequently commissioned from American manufacturers Westinghouse). In due course, it was decided to build four satellites to cater for the full (15 million) passenger projection, with two satellites required in the initial phase of operations. In the event, only two satellites were commissioned, with the second scheduled for 1994 and others following when the airport expanded to its full capacity around 1996.

Even in the early eighties it was clear that Stansted would be a new sort of airport. BAA had created a workable airport at Gatwick, and an above-average building in the shape of North Terminal there. On the other hand, even Norman Payne now admits that Heathrow 4 (opened 1986; architects: Scott, Brownrigg, Turner) had been something of a disappointment. Jane Priestman, who was design director at BAA at the time of the Foster commission, says that appointing Foster was "very much the chairman's decision". Payne, she continues, "had the vision of it: a simple, sensitive building. Terminal 4 had been a disappointment – there was a great pressure to produce something excellent."

Priestman, of course, later moved on to become the Director of Architecture and Design at British Rail, where she was able to exercise a considerable amount of architectural patronage. Her memories of BAA ("compared with BR, a relatively small business… very responsive to managerial initiatives") help to explain the genesis of the Stansted idea.

Norman Payne recalls: "I wanted to know from the start how it would look after five years. We all know that buildings have to change – something always has to be changed or adjusted, and it's the job of those who manage them to adjust things to people's needs." Norman Foster was equally aware from the start that airports are now "discount shopping centres on a grand scale, with the emphasis on emptying your pockets, rather than charging you with the thrill of travel – a sad comparison with the great train stations of the railway age."

Stansted, complete and in operation, is undoubtedly one of the great achievements of late twentieth-century British architecture, and in fact, the only major doubts which still persist concern the nature of Stansted's shops: Have both Normans lost the battle against the shops? Should the solution (and the brief) not have conceded that an airport is a "discount shopping centre"? How much of Stansted's exhilarating open spaces will remain in a decade's time?

# Chapter two

# A pavilion in the landscape

Norman Foster praises Stansted as "a symbol of foresight and prior investment". Perhaps there is an element of irony in that comment in view of the many years of delay before development of the airport began. However, Foster's respect for Sir Norman Payne of BAA is genuine: "BAA has been engineering-led under his chairmanship and that counts for a lot." For everyone involved in the project, Payne was the client: the man who backed the originality of it and made it happen.

Foster's personal passion for flying is well-known. Ultimately it has not, he says, influenced Stansted more than any other of his buildings, but Foster's early sketches for the project underline his interest in "going back to basics". "We drew inspiration from the early days of flying when airfields were very simple affairs. There was always a clear airside and landside so you were never in any doubt where you were." Foster compares many recent airports to digital watches: as far as he is concerned, both are poor communicators. "More and more buildings today are digital. To navigate, say, the Barbican, La Défense, or most big shopping centres – or international airports – is a challenge to mind and body. Digital buildings, with their total dependence on signage and numerical codes, are not really very good at telling you where you are."

Stansted, like so many of our projects, strives for the analogue experience."

The formula "calm, clarity, and convenience" was established early in Foster's work on the project. Norman Foster's own preliminary sketches show a pavilion-like building in which the principle of movement is implicit. There are hints, perhaps, of Mies's National Gallery in Berlin – a glass box on a podium – and of SOM's extraordinary fabric-roofed Haj airport at Jeddah (1981). Even in the early sketches, the roof has an ethereal, undulating quality – suggesting fabric rather than a more solid material – although it was to be three years before the character of the domes was finalised. Foster's Stansted was to be, indeed, a pavilion in the landscape, more dynamic than Mies's Berlin, more permanent than SOM's Jeddah.

Norman Payne comments: "Foster took the concept and developed it – what is most unconventional as a result is the high degree of flexibility." It is clear that Stansted is the crowning achievement of Payne's own career at BAA, and his own ideal of the airport of the future. But it would never have been realised without Norman Foster. Indeed, when Foster made his first presentation to BAA in April 1981, a few months after

One of the prime objectives of Foster's Stansted was to bring back to air travel something of the excitement of the pioneering years – when Heathrow (above) was little more than a collection of tents and, as at Atlanta (top), passengers walked to the aircraft across the tarmac

Foster Associates' formal appointment, he categorically recommended a simple rectangular building on a single level. In so doing, he discarded a number of other BAA options – including one for an L-shaped terminal and for two pavilions (one for arrivals and one for departures) which would be linked by a sort of corridor. During the next year, Foster's concept was developed in detail. The single-level terminal may have been Norman Payne's ideal, but it was obvious that there was a great deal of work to be done before the BAA would be persuaded to select this option above others under consideration. As to the motivating force which would be able to bring the single-level plan to fruition, there was no dispute: it would be Foster Associates.

The architects were, of course, plunged into a planning process which had been under way at BAA for years – an airport is far more than just a terminal. When the architects were appointed, a long and friendly collaboration with BAA's own designers, initially led by Design Director Jane Priestman, subsequently by Dick Petersen, was initiated. Petersen had the advice of the Chairman's Design Group, by no means a toothless body which contained such senior figures in the design world as Helen Robinson, James Pilditch and Professor Frank

Foster rejected the conventional solution of placing services and ducts on the roof in favour of creating a services "undercroft" beneath the concourse. The roof, now lighter and unencumbered, would be less obtrusive in the landscape and allow maximum daylight to illuminate the concourse below

The undercroft contains the British Rail station, baggage-handling systems, the environmental engineering plant, storage and a service road. Passengers proceed through the check-in area, security and immigration controls and departure lounge to a tracked transit station at the same level. From here, passengers are moved by automatic transport vehicles to the satellite buildings, maintaining complete segregation of passengers airside

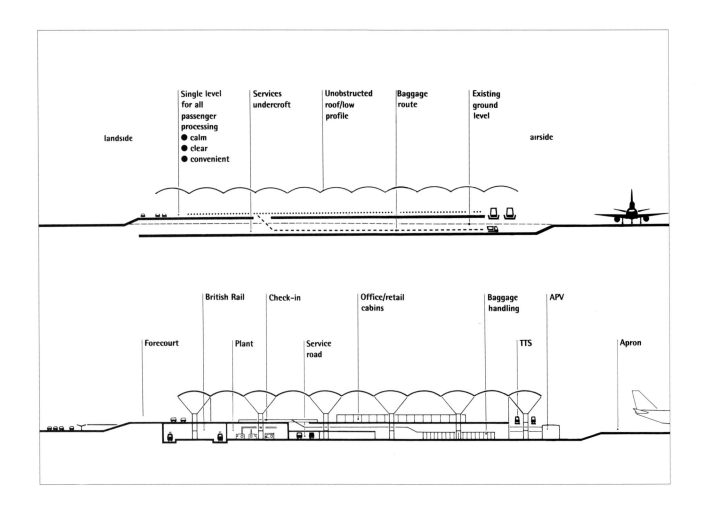

Height. Throughout the process of construction, the Group met at quarterly intervals, mostly on-site and with Sir Norman Payne present, to monitor and comment on Foster's proposals. The meetings were usually cordial, the architects recall, with any serious disagreements having been thrashed out in advance. Only once was there a real confrontation – over Pentagram's novel system of signage – and then Norman Payne was simply adamant that the proposals were to be rejected.

The only planning constraint on the project, in effect, was the size of the site – between the runway and the southern boundary of the airport. However, there were major issues to be decided as to how the site should be used, including the provision of car-parking and the location of the rail link. At Gatwick, the station had been set apart from the airport and given its own identity. There was a danger that Stansted's station would again become a separate British Rail project. Spencer de Grey explains that the architects wanted to give every activity a clearly defined zone within which it could "breathe" – road and rail links had to be rigorously subjected to an overall geometry.

With the basic shape of the building agreed, the idea had to be turned into a reality which could be built. The idea of a well-serviced shed is inherent in all Foster's architecture from IBM at Cosham to the mid-eighties IBM Greenford via Sainsbury Centre and Willis Faber at Ipswich. But there had been nothing on the scale of Stansted, nor – apart from Renault, Swindon – anything as expressive (save, of course, the Hong Kong Bank). But the bank had received publicity in Britain for reasons other than its architectural inventiveness. IBM Greenford had been a notable model of economy and had (Foster believes) influenced BAA's choice of architect. The supposedly high cost of the Hong Kong Bank – which the press had dubbed "the most expensive building in history" – could have become a problem for Foster, although intelligent critics recognised that exceptional buildings do not come cheap. Creating a major building that was also notably economical to build could do the firm no harm at all.

Early on in the planning process, a structural grid of 36 metres was laid down and the architects began to consider how the services could be integrated into the structural system. The idea of the "trees", or a cluster of columns, emerged quite early on, but initially, the air-conditioning plant was to sit on the roof, and this would have required a far beefier structure than the one eventually adopted. The "trees", as they became known,

The Renault Centre in Swindon,
designed by Foster Associates in
1982. The masts create an elegant
landmark – here the umbrellas
which form the roof are supported
from below by structural "trees"

The Renault Centre – the first
of a series of buildings which
used lightweight steel to create
a flexible, open building with an
expressed structure

would have become substantial objects, and potential obstacles to passenger circulation. The element of "clarity", identified by Foster as an essential characteristic, already looked compromised. The services, it was clear, would have to be kept under control.

The height of the building was a critical factor. The typical BAA concourse was about 6 to 9 metres from floor to ceiling, but Foster Associates favoured something far higher. Existing terminals were often a series of small rooms; Stansted on the other hand, was to be one vast room – an internal height of not less than 12 metres was vital if the interior was not to look oppressively low. At the same time, bulk and landscape impact remained a significant issue as the final planning inquiry loomed. The solution was, of course, to invert the traditional approach and locate the services not on the roof but in the basement. In this way, although its final character remained unresolved, the roof itself could be made far less heavy in form – and the structural system could be altogether lighter. All this took some time to resolve. Loren-Butt, who briefly directed the project in its earliest days, before Spencer de Grey returned from Hong Kong, recalls that "it was not until 1982, in fact, that the services went below ground."

Plan and section were developed in tandem. The element of "clarity" – keeping the building simple in form – was never compromised. Transparency and a feeling of direction were associated qualities. After long discussions with BAA's technical staff, it was established that the services would be sited below the concourse, although their exact location was undecided. The architects were keen to keep them within the main "box" and to avoid subsidiary structures.

The nature of the roof would dictate the form of the members supporting it. Fosters worked intensively with structural engineers from Ove Arup & Partners to find the ideal form. As a lightweight steel structure stayed by tension rods, Stansted followed a progression of similar Foster buildings, most notably the Swindon Renault Centre, completed in 1982 and at advanced design stage when Stansted was first considered by the office.

Renault marked a new direction for Foster – a break with the smoothed-off Miesian box and a step in the direction of the romantic Modernism associated with Foster's former partner, Richard Rogers. Working with Martin Manning of Arups, who was to be Arups' project director for Stansted, Foster Associates created a structurally expressive, highly flexible building based

The supports for the roof form
tree-like structures comprising
four interconnected tubular steel
columns. Each dome rises to a
height of 15 metres above the
concourse level. All the distribution
equipment for heating, ventilation,
air-conditioning and lighting for
the concourse is contained within
the clusters of columns

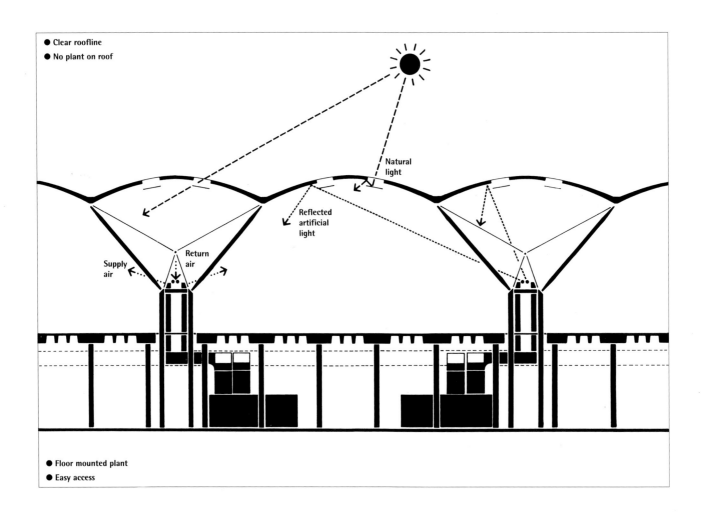

on a 24-metre square grid. The building was designed to contain large areas of racked storage for parts and a high-profile showroom; using a masted, cable-stayed structure was an obvious tactic. In the design of the roof structure – a series of fabricated steel "umbrellas" incorporating roof lights – Renault prefigures Stansted. At Renault, however, the "umbrellas" are suspended from the masts; the structural system had been influenced by Arup's work on the Birmingham Exhibition Centre. Stansted's "domes", a concept really developed during 1984, grow of out the "trees". The structural concept of Stansted is really very simple and very obvious (in marked contrast to earlier terminal buildings at Gatwick and Heathrow), but only emerged in its final form after a long process of discussion and refinement. It is based on the good Victorian principle of cantilevered supports holding up straight spans. The aim was to secure, alongside a striking architectural effect, economy and ease of construction.

If Stansted is, indeed, a "pavilion in the landscape", that image is strengthened by the way the building is dug into its setting. The car-parks, entirely at surface level, were eventually depressed below the forecourt level with access to the building at lower level; the terminal therefore sits in a green setting rather than floating in a sea of asphalt.

The building seizes the advantages of its setting. "It's a building on a hill – optimise", wrote Norman Foster on one of his early sketches. No taller than the average forest tree, the building straddles a natural ridge so that the passenger walking in at road level is at first-floor level by the time he reaches the departure lounge – the main terminal floor is thus at a convenient level for the transit system serving the satellites. The airside road, which serves the baggage hall, is at basement level.

The public inquiry of 1982–83 lasted 258 days. It did not consider architectural details, though the general shape and layout of the terminal was known. During 1982, work at Foster Associates on Stansted slowed down dramatically, although the issue of locating the services was finally – and dramatically – resolved. The design formula existed, but only in February 1984, did detailed work begin in the office: the Stansted project had "taken off". Norman Foster's presentation to BAA on the 8th of that month marked the start of the detailed design process. Foster developed the crucial idea of "transparency": "I am not suggesting necessarily that this is a building which is completely enclosed all the way round with glass and is transparent all the way round," he commented [the transcription is the office's...],

Lifts, ramps and escalators bring
passengers from the railway station,
coach station and car-park directly
up to the concourse level. The
vehicular drop-off on the forecourt
is at concourse level, beneath the
sheltering overhang of the great roof

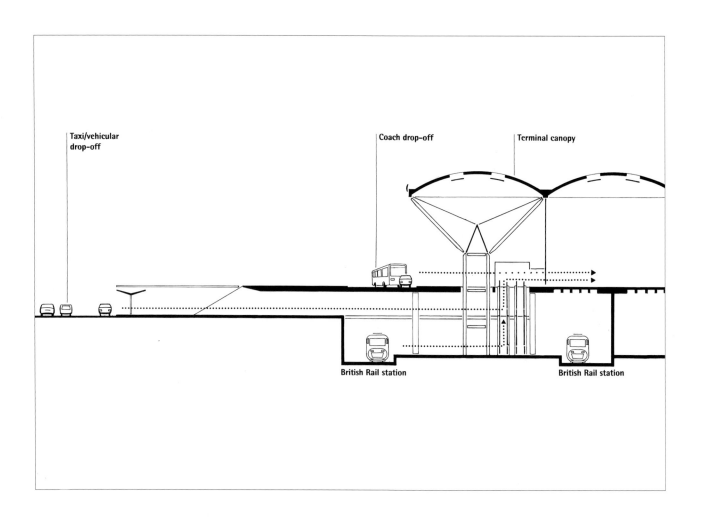

Taxi/vehicular
drop-off

Coach drop-off

Terminal canopy

British Rail station

British Rail station

"but it would be transparent where it was important to guide you.... Again, as you move through, there is always this relationship between where you are actually going and the aircraft. That dialogue between the aircraft and runways and the landscape – quite carefully controlled views".... The building, Foster urged, should be "essentially... a very calm object in the landscape".

"A strong visual identity," Foster suggested, was vital. The essence of that identity already existed, but now had to be fleshed out. A study model from early 1984 depicts a flat roof. The glazing system in this model is quite unresolved – the blank Miesian wall lingers here. By the end of the year the dome idea had been developed in detail. The Technical Studies Report of November 1983 had outlined a number of options for the configuration of the services-free roof, including a fabric covering. All options allowed for roof lights – essential in a naturally-lit, low-energy building. It was to be yet another element in the tree-and-dome assemblage which, in effect, is Stansted – the steel forest, with its glazed crown....

The November 1983 report, the outcome of intense consultation between client, architects and engineers, paved the way for detailed designs and was a vital stage in the succession of actions Norman Foster had laid down in an early sketch: "Identify solution; engineer solution; document; build; use." At this period, a four-year construction programme was envisaged, with opening scheduled for 1990. The essential character of the structure had now been established: how could it be built? Energy considerations were, of course, vitally important, and fire engineering had to be given a high priority.

The look of the building could still at this stage have varied considerably as the integration of the cladding with the structure was explored. Should it follow the line of the trees, canting forward or backward with dramatically expressive effect? If so, the nature of the "trees" and the roof itself would need to be adjusted. In retrospect, the choice of vertical cladding, with the trees emerging through at the edges of the enclosure, seems inevitable – providing an "infinite" quality which reflects Foster's post-Hong Kong desire for "calm" above drama – but the other options had to be fully considered. Arups had produced a diagram showing the 36-metre Stansted grid imposed on a section of Paddington Station. The main spans of the train-sheds are only a little short of 36 metres. It was the same balance of engineering and art which was central to the work of the Victorian engineers that the designers of Stansted now sought to achieve.

# Chapter three

# Raising the roof

Once the basic structure had been
determined, Foster Associates
built numerous models to study
how best to solve the complex
problem of the external cladding.
In this rejected solution the cladding
completely encloses the structure

Another model illustrates the first
steps towards the final design in
which a row of trees sit outside the
enclosed area. This has the advantage
of sheltering the vertical glazed wall
from solar gain and providing
weather protection for drop-off

A single level, clearly planned, rectangular building (a big box) with all of its services concealed in an undercroft and with a lightweight, transparent structure based on structural trees supporting a top-lit roof – this was to be Norman Foster's Stansted. Basic section and plan had been established before the final public inquiry. The government's eventual approval of the project in 1985 – the grant of outline planning permission for, in effect, "a rectangle on a piece of paper" – had implications for the shape of the terminal.

Initially, the new terminal would provide for eight million passengers a year, with the possibility, subject to parliamentary approval, of an extension in a second phase of construction to cater for 15 million. The original commission had envisaged a full-size terminal, initially fitted out to cater for only half its capacity, the strategy employed at Gatwick North. What has been built is inevitably a little unbalanced – the full symmetry will only emerge with phase 2. With the terminal cut in size, it was decided to build just two satellites in the first phase, and the order for rapid transit cars was reduced. In the event, the two-stage building programme has accorded well with commercial realities. Economic recession, combined with the Gulf War of early 1991 brought about a notable downturn in air traffic. But nobody believes this will be more than a temporary blip in a steadily rising graph. The building strategy had altered, but the basic principles did not change.

When the final scheme went to the local planning committee in February 1986 it was passed in 30 seconds. Spencer de Grey says that he half expected the detailed planning stages to be used by objectors in their attempts to delay the project – "it would have been a predictable tactic, but no objections were raised." In the spring of 1986 BAA was already on site, building the new road network. The aim was to start building a year later in order to finish on schedule by the end of 1990 and open the terminal early in 1991.

Martin Manning of Ove Arup & Partners had worked with Foster Associates as project director at the Renault Centre, a landmark building for the practice. Arups were therefore called in at an early stage of the Stansted commission (February 1981) to advise on the feasibility of ideas which Norman Foster had already been developing for the form of the terminal. "The single-level terminal was very much Norman Foster's choice," says Manning, who saw clearly that the slope of the sight made a one-level building, with a undercroft below to

contain the services, not only feasible but also extremely logical. (In fact, with the excavation of the site, the natural slope has been increased and now no part of the completed terminal is actually "underground". The BAA planners, says Manning, were hard to convince – a point which Loren Butt reinforces. "At first, they were simply very inflexible," he says.

According to Manning, initially there were thoughts of a cable-hung structure. But whereas Fleetguard and Renault had been essentially warehouses, full of goods rather than people and relatively uninteresting internally, an airport was a public building – the traveller should enjoy something of the structural drama. The structure would be contained within the building envelope; in effect it would form the architecture. Very quickly, thoughts turned towards a "mushroom" structure supporting the roof – the initial inspiration came from Frank Lloyd Wright's Johnson Wax Building, says Manning. Johnson Wax was one of the buildings which, seen in magazines, had encouraged Norman Foster to train as an architect, and had also played a part in the evolution of the Hong Kong Bank design. The next stage was the concept of the "trees": thirty-six of them growing out of the structural towers and set at 36-metre intervals. At first, the trees were to be completely free-standing of the concrete slab floor (of which they are, of course, structurally independent, since they sit on the floor of the undercroft), necessitating expansion joints in the roof. Using the floor to prop the trees made for a simpler roof solution, minus expansion joints.

The trees are not only the key to the structure of Stansted but also represent a major attraction of the building for the client seeking economy and rapid construction. By assembling the basic structure first and then adding the roof decking, a covered shell was provided in which the task of casting the terminal floor and inserting all the other elements of the building could proceed under cover. This key part of the strategy for Stansted was one of the elements which convinced BAA that the Foster approach was exactly in line with their own requirements.

The exact form of the trees then had to be decided. Manning still feels that the "branches" should perhaps have sprung out from floor level ("like a Christmas tree"), rather than squatting as they do on 12-metre-high square bases. The next engineering decision to be made was the character of the roof covering – eventually resolved as lightweight latticed domes (18 square metres) which

consisted of intersecting barrel vaults, sitting on the trees. The idea of the domes came from the charismatic engineer, Peter Rice. This solution, linked to prefabricated construction techniques, was to be invaluable in the strategy of rapid construction. "We originally wanted the cladding and the structure to be one surface," recalls Manning. "The clad shells were a compromise idea, but very economical."

Having created a vast roofscape – at 200 square metres, twice the size of Lord's Cricket Ground – the matter of drainage then had to be tackled. The penetration of the building by a series of downpipes was obviously unacceptable. It was equally obvious that the drainage system could not utilise the service pods (which do not touch the roof). What was required was a totally, one-hundred percent reliable drainage system which would ensure against blocking and flooding. In the end, a syphonic, negative-pressure system of the type which has been widely used in Germany and Scandinavia for many years was chosen. A total of 121 horizontal pipes, which run east–west along the roof, feed 16 downpipes located at each end of the building. All the low-diameter (100 mm) pipes are made of stainless steel – the system is designed to be low maintenance.

The roof during construction in 1987. It is 198 metres square and some 15 metres high, supported by 36 free-standing groups of columns which rise from ground level and pass through the concourse floor. The roof shells were assembled on the ground and lifted into position complete

Martin Manning has an engineer's reservations about the final form of some of the steelwork, but even he will admit that the so-called "Jesus nut" at the apex of the roof towers, rigidly fixing branches, grid-beams and tension rods, was a remarkably practical success. The steel erectors discovered that it was essentially a self-correcting mechanism, bracing all the components and producing an exactness of lines in the building. And the origins of its name? "The idea came from a friend of mine in the RAF," Manning explains. "The Jesus nut is what holds on the rotor blades on a Lynx helicopter – if it were to fail, you'd be saying your prayers! I mentioned the thing to Norman Foster who, with his interest in helicopters, found it irresistible."

Stansted is, in engineering terms, says Manning, "interesting rather than radically innovative". The technology had been explored at previous Foster jobs. The language of the structure started with Renault, but was refined at Stansted, the ultimate Foster enclosure. Stansted is an all-round work of architecture: the structure provides for a complex interaction of activities, human and mechanical. In the end, the origins of everything there lie in the architectural decisions taken on the division between people and services.

The building now had a structure – undercroft, concrete floor (an *in situ* coffered slab), "trees", roof – which would make Foster's concept work. Foster Associates now moved on to the many detailed design decisions which would make Stansted an integrated, consistent, satisfying work of architecture. By early 1984 the general external look of the terminal had been largely resolved: it would be contained within vertical glass walls which, in accord with the overall grid, would be set 18 metres behind the edge of the roof – a decision which also helped to reduce solar gain. Cladding had to take into account significant constraints imposed by structural movement, solar gain and windloadings, while aesthetic ambitions for "lots of glass" and towards "transparency" and clarity had to be tempered by considerations of the availability of both materials and fixing methods.

The Technical Studies Report of November 1983, in some ways an exercise to keep the momentum of the project going while a final go-ahead was awaited, looked at all the cladding options for the 17,000-square-metre envelope of the terminal: How should the cladding be supported? From the ground? Should it be suspended from the roof? Could it be linked to the main "tree" structure? Energy and maintenance considerations were also to the fore: economy, the architects insist, was always high on the agenda for this job. Double-glazing was obviously essential, both for energy conservation and to exclude aircraft noise. As executed, the glazing of the concourse is fixed into the concrete floor slab – which has expansion joints – and tied into the roof (which has no expansion joints). The roof has to be able to move with wind pressure: a conundrum. The solution was ingenious: the glazing mullions to the roof would be connected with a flexible link, bearing on a horizontal stainless steel rod.

Stansted as conceived by Norman Foster ten years ago was a pure, transparent box. The completed building has fully transparent walls (shaded by the overhanging canopies) on the arrivals (south) and landside (north) elevations, but on the other elevations the glazing has evolved as two-thirds translucent, with clear panels only at the lower levels to achieve the necessary solar shading. Yet if anything, this has increased the strong directional pull of the building from entrance front to airstrip.

Natural light is *the* key element in Foster's architecture: managed, utilised but in the end invading and flooding the structure. Using natural light also makes sense – people are happier in naturally lit buildings. Reducing artificial lighting saves money. At Stansted, the aim was to make daylighting adequate during all daytime hours and artificial lighting essential only after dark. Initially, this was to be achieved by inserting long, narrow strips of glazing between the panels of the roof. But with the advent of the tree and dome roof it was possible to incorporate the roof-lights within the main roof modules in a satisfyingly logical way which recalls the approach at Renault.

The roof lights as constructed consist of four triangular roof lights in each 18-square-metre roof shell – 11 square metres of glazing in each shell. The metal mesh daylight reflectors suspended beneath the roof lights have a dual role. First, they diffuse direct sunlight and reduce solar gain on bright days. Secondly, they reflect the artificial lighting directed upward from the trees at night. The reflectors avoid the impression that the great roof is full of black "holes" after dark.

The 36-square-metre structural grid was the basis for the integration of the services. Half the total cost of the terminal went to that part of it, below the concourse floor, which the public never sees – the secret core of the place, like the crypt of a Gothic cathedral. The undercroft grew in size gradually. Once the principle of below-floor servicing was established – against the ingrained practice of BAA's engineers – it extended under most of the concourse. But

The undercroft of the terminal contains the mechanical services – principally the air-handling plant and the baggage-handling system. They are carefully organised to avoid confusion: ducting for major services runs north–south; minor services run east–west

it was only when, late in the project, the railway station was incorporated into the terminal that the undercroft assumed its present form. Chillers, airhandling, electrical plant and boilers were concentrated in the southern half of the 9-metre-high undercroft, feeding upwards through the structural trees. Waffle slab concrete allowed the services to penetrate the floor without impairing its structural performance. "We gradually got BAA's engineers behind us," says Loren Butt, who headed work on the services for Foster. "We decided that a fresh start was vital to avoid the messy confusion typical of earlier terminals. We met resistance, but we persisted – and gradually the BAA people began to see the sense of the approach."

Stansted is a product of the new concern – as much among architects as clients – to create economical, energy-conscious buildings. Waste heat from the concourse area should generally be sufficient to warm the building in winter, except in the most extreme cold. The northern sector of the undercroft, towards the runway, was given over to a major airport activity: baggage handling. The lower-level baggage hall is a huge space, equipped with a supermarket-style optical scanner which automatically directs baggage to the correct flight (there is a full back-up manual system, in

case of failure). Trucks load directly from the undercroft to transfer baggage to the aircraft.

The structure of Stansted, containing about 2,800 tons of steel, was designed for rapid construction. The towers were prefabricated off-site (by the highly experienced Tubeworkers of Warwickshire, who had worked on Renault), brought in by road and lifted on to their concrete bases by crane (the first of them arrived on site in February, 1987). The "branches" were then fixed on and prestressed by tightening the "Jesus nuts". The 18-square-metre roof shells were next simply dropped into place with their aluminium decking already in place. With the roof in position, it was possible (by late 1987) to begin casting the concourse floor. Cladding and fitting out then followed.

Some of the most impressive photographs taken of the building date from the period, towards the end of 1987, when the "bones" of Stansted were in place and the full majesty of the structure, as a work of engineering and architecture, could be appreciated. The idea had become reality – Foster's "big shed" had arrived in Essex and now had to be transformed into a place where people could check in, eat, drink, go to the lavatory, buy a bottle of duty-free whisky or a hamburger and generally cope with the fraught business of taking an air journey.

# Chapter four

# The poetry
# of lighting

The British Rail station is at
undercroft level, built of in-situ
concrete rather than steel and glass.
Its massive, well-lit flanking wall
forms one edge of the great platform
on which the terminal floor sits

Check-in desks, security gates, passport controls, customs posts, baggage carousels, lavatories, baby-changing facilities, a chapel, bars, cafes, public telephones, a small supermarket (duty-free), news-stands and other shops, plus behind-the-scenes administrative and security offices – and lots of people. Norman Foster's idea of a return to the early days of flying was, in some senses, always doomed to failure. Passengers are rarely allowed to walk across the airstrip to their aircraft in large modern airports. The very act of flying is complex. Boarding a plane today can mean leaving home at 6 a.m. to take off at 10 a.m. for a one-hour flight; if you can pass through the airport in two hours, you are very lucky. The heroic days of flying – the age of the tent on the airfield – are long departed.

Yet Stansted was consciously designed to evoke those heroic days when the airport represented the beginning of an adventure rather than the setting for a bureaucratic-cum-commercial process. A return to primitive simplicity had to be, as ever, a vision. Reality is different: air travel is now for the masses. Skies are congested; there are delays, and occasionally there are worse incidents like the bomb which destroyed an airliner over the Scottish town of Lockerbie. No one actually believes there is much prospect of air travel becoming less fraught and complicated.

Foster's client, BAA, no longer a public service, is by its own admission engaged in a "long-term investment business". In the paper *The Impact of Commercialisation on the Planning and Engineering of Airports*, delivered to the Institution of Civil Engineers in December 1990, A.R. Westbrook and D.H. Williams of BAA (the latter, Stansted's Development Director) spelt it out: "Shopping generally is a fashion business...BAA wants its new terminals to reflect this and increasingly, BAA has moved to concessionaire-funded fit-out to reflect the 'short life' fashion nature of concessions". The authors concluded ominously: "One thing is certain, whatever was planned and often agreed will always be likely to change in operation...."

Norman Foster angered the BAA when, at Foster Associates' own completion party held in the baggage hall a few days before public opening, he complained that the place was already being spoiled and that the lager-advert umbrellas would probably soon arrive. As architect, he would have argued for a far more influential role, even after the building had been handed over.

Foster had been commissioned – against the odds – to design the terminal in total: structure, services, and interior. The interior fit-out flowed from, and was integrated into, the structure rather than being a superimposed layer. A great deal of thought, for example, went into the design of the structural trees so that all the requisite services could be contained within them. Spencer de Grey recalls long discussions about the trees' detailed design so that they could be kept clear of protruding pipes and ducts. As well as handling air distribution and incorporating flight information screens, loudspeakers, clocks, signs and firefighting points, the trees were the location points for the terminal's artificial lighting.

The trees are the keys to Stansted. They support the entire main structure – the concourse floor stands on its own concrete columns – and they convey the services from undercroft to concourse, linking sources of heat, fresh air and power with the users. Fresh-air pipes are grouped around a return air-duct (which also serves as a smoke vent in case of fire). The uplighters sit on top of the supply ducts and the other services are grouped around the edge of the pod. It is a remarkably logical, elegant way of handling the diverse services which are needed in a large public space such as an airport terminal. At Stansted, the centre of the trees contains a service stair; if anything goes wrong, it can be dealt with behind the scenes.

By day, Stansted is filled with natural light through the walls and roof lights. By night, it is lit not from above, but by a series of uplighters mounted on the trees and light reflecting down from the ceiling – a logical corollary of the rejection of overhead servicing but a device initially resisted by BAA engineers. Norman Foster spoke early in the project of the building "glowing" in the dark. Writing of Stansted in the forthcoming edition of his personal sketches (Norman Foster Sketches, edited by Werner Blaser, Birkhauser), Foster comments that the poetry of the lighting had to match the poetry of the engineering: "However, the lighting is a different kind of poetry, more of the heart. It is always shifting and elusive...." These qualities had to be present by night as much as by day – an airport is a 24-hour building.

Something more than conventional floodlighting was needed and Foster went to an established collaborator, American lighting consultant Claude Engle, for the design of the system. Engle's lights, made by Erco, use special reflectors to project the light in a wide diagonal sweep. The approach stops short of being overly dramatic; rather, it enhances the overall "calm" which was always an intrinsic quality of the building. Flexible and responsive to changing external light conditions, the system also meets the demands for economy in operation which were never far from the minds of the architects. Combined

Ramps leading to the main concourse
provide access from the railway
station, bus station and car-parks

with abundant task-lighting, it produces an effect which Spencer de Grey justly claims is "both spectacular and very cheerful".

A great glass shed full of light.... But a shed equally full of people. Flexibility was demanded of the building – the potential to economically accommodate change and rearrangement. Here seemed to lie the best hope of coming to terms with the shops and the offices, and the lavatories and the bars. Check-in and baggage reclaim facilities had to be anchored to the baggage handling system, but all other internal activities could be contained within the overall grid in a series of Foster-designed "cabins" floating within the "enormous room" of the terminal. Sitting on the concourse floor in the manner of independent, portable Foster buildings based on a secondary 1.2-metre planning grid, these structures would have their own fire and environmental controls.

The cabins could be seen as buildings within a building – yet they have always been part of the design; indeed, the design is inconceivable without them. An enormous open space has great attractions, but equally it has its own problems. One of the most compelling problems is the provision of fire security. With restaurants, kitchens and shops full of highly flammable goods (including thousands of litres of spirits in the duty-free shop) there is an obvious need for sophisticated fire engineering. However, if the shops, bars and restaurants enclosed within the cabins are excluded, the problem is vastly reduced. This has been accomplished by compartmentalising the cabins – providing fire shutters and sprinkler systems for each unit, and isolating them from the main space. Seen in this context, the cabins are a vital part of the Foster strategy for Stansted. What the architects could not entirely control, however, is what some would feel is the rather banal quality of the shop fascias. Go beyond a Foster front, and you could be in any shop in any UK high street.

There are aspects of the interior which seem a little at odds with the undeniable grandeur of the architecture. Norman Foster likes to draw parallels between the building and the great railway termini of the last century. But there are also important differences. Paddington and King's Cross are essentially sheds for trains: hard-edged, semi-external places where the winds blow in, with clearly subsidiary spaces for people. At an airport, the machines are outside – the terminal is an insulated box, double-glazed against noise and clearly "inside". Yet the simple elegance of the building carries all before it – you are happy to be a participant in Foster's game. At once

The structural tree acts as a
triumphal archway and a front
door to passengers arriving at the
drop-off forecourt at concourse
level. Overleaf: Looking back to
the terminal from the satellite

remarkably straightforward and subtly evocative, the
building ends up a celebration of the act of flying.

One of the most satisfying aspects of the terminal is
the overall flooring – extending into both the British Rail
station and the rapid transit stations – in grey Italian
granite. Beautifully finished and laid in a sand bed on
the concrete slab of the concourse to counter possible
movement, it is practical and has the right characteristics
of integrity and durability. Beyond the security barriers the
departure lounge is carpeted, a requirement on which BAA
would not compromise, and one which typifies its ideas on
"passenger comfort". But did it have to be extended over
the entire departure area? Designed by Ron Nixon, its grey,
black and white pattern is discreet – ideas of including
elements of strong colour were rejected by Foster, who felt
that its restless quality would be at odds with the
building's calm. In contrast, the passenger seating (Tecno),
check-in desks and screens (some of them making good
use of "fritted" glass, are all solid and appropriate.

The tranquillity of the whole interior, it was assumed,
would be underpinned by the palette of Foster colours
throughout: varying shades of grey and white. It was Alan
Fletcher of Pentagram who remarked tartly that "Fosters
seem to think that grey is a colour." Pentagram (who had

worked with Richard Rogers at Lloyd's) were brought in by Foster Associates to advise on the vital issue of signage in the building. BAA already had a standard signage system – black lettering on a yellow background – developed in the 1960s by Jock Kinneir, which it was anxious not to abandon. "We told them clearly that they had to have our standard system," says Sir Norman Payne, yet the instructions could not have been very clear. Somehow, Fletcher and his colleagues were allowed to work up an alternative approach, including the use of giant directional arrows, numbers and pictograms which were as unacceptable to Norman Foster as they were to Norman Payne. When the proposals were put to BAA they were turned down flat. The 1960s system, Pentagram were informed, was inviolable. A compromise was worked up by Pentagram and Foster Associates. The black-on-yellow look remains, but the signs are at least integrated into the architecture of the structural towers and are based on a clear module – one line per slat, with lettering always justified to the left – while reduced versions of the "supergraphics" have appeared in the terminal to mark toilets, eating places and other basic facilities.

It is ironic that so much debate took place over the signing of a building where signing had been deemed almost irrelevant. The passenger, it had been assumed, would find his way easily through a terminal notable for its uncluttered clarity. However, as the building has been fitted out, the clarity has been somewhat diluted. BAA felt that despite the straightforward nature of a building, passengers still looked to signs for reassurance. The clearest view through the building is on the arrivals side. The departing passenger is unlikely to see the plane in which he is to fly – unless he arrives late and catches a glimpse of it taking off! In part, this is because the second of the satellite buildings – directly in front of the terminal – is not yet complete. But there are other problems. Leaving aside the (inevitable) intrusion of the cabins, the barrier between landside and airside is critical. The arriving passenger immediately comes into a very large space, so that the intrusion of opaque glass screens at the Customs point does not jar. But from the opposite side, it slices the building off dramatically. On the departures side, fritted glass makes a less solid barrier.

The passenger will also see the top of the stained glass tower, which marks the main cafeteria area. The tower was designed by the artist Brian Clarke, whose previous architectural commissions include work with Arata Isozaki in Japan and a massive shopping-centre project in Leeds.

Although the architect's aim was to create a building through which passengers could easily find their way, there was considerable debate about signs and graphics. Pentagram wanted a conspicuous signage system. Foster Associates wanted to integrate graphic signs with the architecture and BAA wanted to reassure passengers with its standard black and yellow system

Brian Clarke's tower of stained
glass is a beacon at the centre of
the building, giving a focus to the
cafeteria concessions and shops,
their basic discipline somewhat
compromised by variegated signage

At one point, there was discussion of Clarke also doing a long coloured panel in one of the external walls. That would have been costly – and perhaps too demonstrative. The tower, accompanied by a series of back-lit wall panels, was the more practical alternative: Stansted's largest piece of "public art". Admirable in itself, the tower has the disadvantage of breaking into the clear space above the cabins, another complicating intrusion into an essentially simple building.

The first satellite completed continues the aesthetic of the main building. Passengers transfer from the terminal via the tracked transit system and arrive in a station below the satellite. Escalators and lifts carry them up to the top floor, an open lounge with fine views of the runway. They go down a level to board aircraft through linkbridges – agreeably high-tech looking devices. Arriving passengers descend immediately to the TTS (Track Transit System) station. The satellites, alas, cannot be as simple as the terminal itself. For security reasons, arriving and departing passengers must be strictly segregated – a certain element of complexity in the circulation system is unavoidable.

The Stansted railway station might well not have been designed by Foster Associates at all. Jane Priestman confirms that at first, British Rail intended to have the station designed in-house, but she pushed for Foster to be given the job. The initial idea was to keep the station apart, a clearly absurd plan that dated from the period when Stansted was to consist of two separate terminal buildings. Later, when the station was brought into the undercroft – Norman Payne says that he insisted on the change – some degree of continuity was therefore needed in the treatment of terminal and station. The same granite paving extends across both, but the station has a railway ambience, solid and inevitably monumental. Platforms are contained by a 500-metre-long retaining wall which, says Martin Manning, represents one of the most notable engineering achievements on the site. Linked to the concourse by ramps and lifts, it shares a common trolley system – a notable advance for luggage-laden travellers and made possible by slightly inclining platform edges to prevent trolleys tumbling on to the tracks.

For all the compromises, the disagreements and, it has to be said, the disfigurements, Stansted is a Foster building through and through. Moreover, it is the first major Foster building, after a string of corporate headquarters, cultural institutions and straightforward sheds, which has had to come to terms with the naked force of commerce. So far it has survived the encounter.

# Chapter five

# A vision at work

"It demonstrates that you can take a traditionally complex building type and do something new with it that captures people's imaginations, *and* do that on a tight commercial budget." For Norman Foster, this is where the essential quality of Stansted lies. He adds: "It also demonstrates how services can be gently – virtually invisibly – integrated into a building. It uses natural light in a joyful way. It evokes a traditional architectural language without any recourse to applied period devices. Lastly, it fits easily into the landscape. Stansted shows that you can do all these things without being at all apologetic or compromising."

Stansted is a landmark in the history of an architectural practice whose reputation, in Britain and abroad, has never stood higher. In one sense, it is the apotheosis of a building form – the superior shed – which Foster Associates have made peculiarly their own and which, the Hong Kong Bank notwithstanding, provides a continuing image for the office. Equally, it is a pioneering public building, looking forward to the rail terminal at King's Cross which could finally put Norman Foster's stamp on the face of central London.

In their own distinctive fashion, the progression of works which point the way to the Stansted achievement is clear enough: Willis Faber (energy-conscious, and one of the first Modernist buildings of its generation to be genuinely contextual), the Sainsbury Centre (lofty and low-energy), Renault, Swindon (the structural precursor), IBM, Greenford (economical and rapidly constructed). Interestingly, Norman Foster compares Stansted with a very early work designed with Team 4, the now-demolished Reliance Controls Factory at Swindon (1967). "Nobody sees the parallels, but Reliance was an extraordinarily dainty building where the services somehow disappeared into the structure."

"Stansted is a building which is hard to date," says Foster. "It has this quality of calm and repose." Foster was never content to be labelled a "high-tech" architect, pointing out that even at the Hong Kong Bank the structure and services are integrated rather than flaunted.

Was the single-level terminal designed in a mood of mistaken optimism? Would it have been better to tuck away the shops on another level (the two-level formula)? Would Richard Rogers adopt this same arrangement for Heathrow 5? "Have two levels," says Foster, "and you'd have two levels of commerce – a day spent with BAA would teach you that." Foster is uncompromising in his assertion that Stansted was the outcome of a "vision". "It wasn't the outcome of rational discussions or of putting

The convenience of the single-level
concourse is a very real advantage
to the passenger with laden trolley
in the baggage reclaim hall, as well
as to the handicapped traveller

things through a computer – there was an architectural vision at work." It was a vision that survived scrutiny by a client which was a hardened operator, always conscious of its duties to the public, though ever mindful that it must also function successfully as a commercial concern. Stansted could not have happened without Norman Payne, in particular, who always backed Foster and helped to overcome the natural conservatism of a large corporate body. Foster's terminal, costing about £100 million, is part of a much bigger, £400 million development of the airport and was one element in a strategy to cater for an estimated 100 million passengers a year at London's three airports in the early years of next century.

Yet, as the generator of ideas and the true design leader of the terminal project, the Foster office indeed created that part of Stansted which, celebrated as architecture, provides an image for the entire airport. Suggestions that the architects are mere facilitators, giving form to someone else's ideas, are resented at Foster Associates. "It was a huge educational task," says Foster, "convincing people that it could be done this way."

Parallels with the published designs for King's Cross are obvious. The rail terminal would be a tall, glazed pavilion, with a lightweight roof structure, though probably without air conditioning. Stansted is a low-energy building – recycling heat in winter alone saves half a million kilowatts of electricity a year. Could the terminal have been done without air conditioning, making use of natural ventilation? Probably not, says Spencer de Grey, since airport noise levels make air vents impractical. "But I am sure you could turn off the chillers even in the hottest weather and still have tolerable conditions simply through the circulation of air." On light summer evenings very little artificial lighting is required – the artificial environment is capable of being finely tuned. As an energy-saving building, as much as in its sturdy contextualism, Stansted is "new-tech" rather than "high-tech".

Its "calm" – the word to which Norman Foster returns again and again when discussing the project – is far removed from the expressive drama of Rogers', Lloyds, or even the Gothic gauntness of Foster's Renault, the building which was something of a testing-ground for Stansted. Would the word "calm" epitomise the certain smoothing-over, the softness, seen in Foster's work – for example in the ITN building, the office and apartment block at Battersea and the forthcoming contribution to the Terry Farrell-planned Chiswick Park? While expressiveness and experimentation (and even disorder

Using the BAA sign manual, a new system was developed to integrate with the building. Each message is conveyed on a single line highlighted by the use of a rear-illuminated slat. To help identify certain key facilities – toilets, restaurants and bureaux de change – large pictograms are used

and *Angst*) characterise the new modern architecture of the 1990s throughout the world, Foster seems to be seeking an ever-greater refinement. Is he leaving Richard Rogers and a bevy of younger firms to blaze new trails? Has fastidiousness replaced innovation? Is the suppression of servicing paralleled by the suppression of emotion?

This analysis is less than just. Norman Foster has spoken eloquently of the social and environmental role of architecture. His interest in the achievements of the nineteenth century is genuine – comparing Stansted to a Victorian railway terminus is no mere conceit. "Heroic" is the other adjective Foster uses to describe Stansted. In nineteenth century terms, he wants to be a W. H. Barlow (engineer of the St Pancras train shed) rather than a Gilbert Scott (architect of the elaborate St Pancras Hotel). As a Modernist – he does not fear the term – Foster is wary of obviously monumental gestures. In the United States, Saarinen created romantically Modern airport terminals in New York and Washington. Rogers' preliminary study for Heathrow 5 takes the inspiration for its sweeping roof from Aalto. But Foster pursues another course: the inevitability of engineering and pragmatic experiment. Study the options, test them out, verify their practicability, identify the ideal – then build it. This is the Foster way –

Signs have been designed as
a modular slat system so that
they can be easily and flexibly
integrated into the architectural
fabric of the building

practical but never prosaic. The unique (for Britain at least) commission given to Foster to design the entire terminal, including services and interior, has produced a totality which nothing can undo. Foster and his colleagues may complain about the potted plants and re-arranged furniture, but that soaring space – up to 11 metres tall above the cabin roofs – is, and will remain, inviolate.

Stansted, like every radical building, invites the question: could it have been even more uncompromising? Could the servicing, for example, have been simplified by eliminating traditional boilers and opting for an all-electric system? Could the whole departures process have been simplified far more, without sacrificing security? Why the carpet? Why the incongruous retail fascias? From issues of basic design to those of detail, all of these questions reflect uncertainty about the definition of an air terminal. Is it a public building? Is it a shopping centre from which aircraft depart? For that matter, is Foster's client, BAA, a public utility or a commercial developer? Under Norman Payne's leadership, BAA has tried, with some success, to be both.

Foster has no doubt that Stansted is the first of a new generation of terminal buildings. It is, in his words, an "analogue building" which can be easily "read" and comprehended. It represents for him an expression of the liberation of technology. Foster Associates designed their earlier serviced sheds in the most economical way: using identical, mass-produced, uniform components. Now it is possible to produce one-off building components at reasonable cost; the architect has been liberated. "The move away from those more generalised solutions also marks a growing dissatisfaction on our part with their limitations and a quest for richer and more sculptural spaces", comments Foster.

Stansted remains the most striking product in this country of that "quest". It stands as a key monument in the rebirth of a modern architecture which, conscious of the needs of man and of the natural world, responds with a balance of the romantic and the rational which is the essence of all great architecture. "The building is a vision", Norman Foster has said. However, he recognises that the building is there because the vision was translated into the process of design and construction: "It can be questioned, assailed, revered – but it is only there because of teamwork which at every turn rejected the shortcut, the lazy way out and instead collectively burned the midnight oil." The words sum up the way in which great architecture is conceived and realised.

# Photographs
# and drawings

Right: Each 18-square-metre roof
shell includes four triangular
openings which flood the concourse
with suffused daylight. The plan area
of the floor, at 39,200 square metres,
is equivalent to six football pitches

Previous pages: Approaching
the terminal by road; Stansted
terminal from the car-park

Left: Foster's approach to
rainwater disposal is typically
inventive – and practical.
A trouble-free but unobtrusive
system was required. The selected
syphonic system consists of a
specially designed outlet with
horizontal pipes running east-
west delivering water to the
edge of the roof, from where it
runs through exposed downpipes,
tapering at their base

Below: Tecno's standard seating
range was modified to meet BAA's
demanding standards

The fully glazed ramp connecting with the station and the short-term car-park and the coach station – the enclosure is designed for maximum transparency and consists of single sheets of toughened glass bolted to the steel structure

Right: interiors reflect the uncluttered approach adopted throughout the terminal. The colours are natural greys and white: strong colour is only used to highlight information required by passengers, such as direction signs and flight information

Domestic departures

Domestic arrivals

→ International departures

→ Desks 97 to 100

HM customs  VAT enquiries

Chapel

→ Restaurants & bar

→ Shops

Emergency exit

Previous page: Roof lights admit
enough natural light for most
purposes, and even on an overcast
day, the energy-saving advantages
are obvious – it is rarely necessary
to use overall artificial lighting
in daytime

Left: Brian Clarke's colourful
totem pole in the heart of the
concourse creates a contrast
with the restrained colour scheme
of the rest of the building

Below: Foster Associates, as interior
and product designers for the project
as well as architects, designed
many of the elements, including
the cabins for offices, toilets, duty-
free and catering, the check-in
islands, litter bins and glazed screens

Satellite 1 is the first of the two
satellites required to meet the
8 million passenger per annum
through-flow. The three-storey
building is 250 metres long.
At concourse level the external
skin consists of a double-glazed
curtain walling system using
green tinted glass

The concourse level open gate
lounge with a central roof-light that
runs the full length of the building

The Jesus nut, at the apex of roof
towers, was found to be a self-
correcting mechanism, bracing
all the components and producing
an exactness of lines

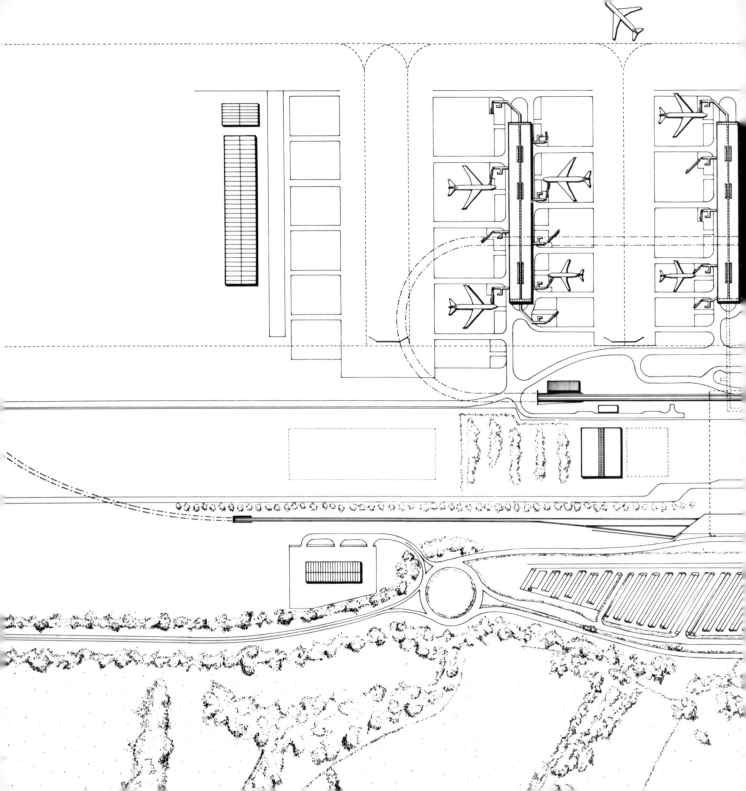

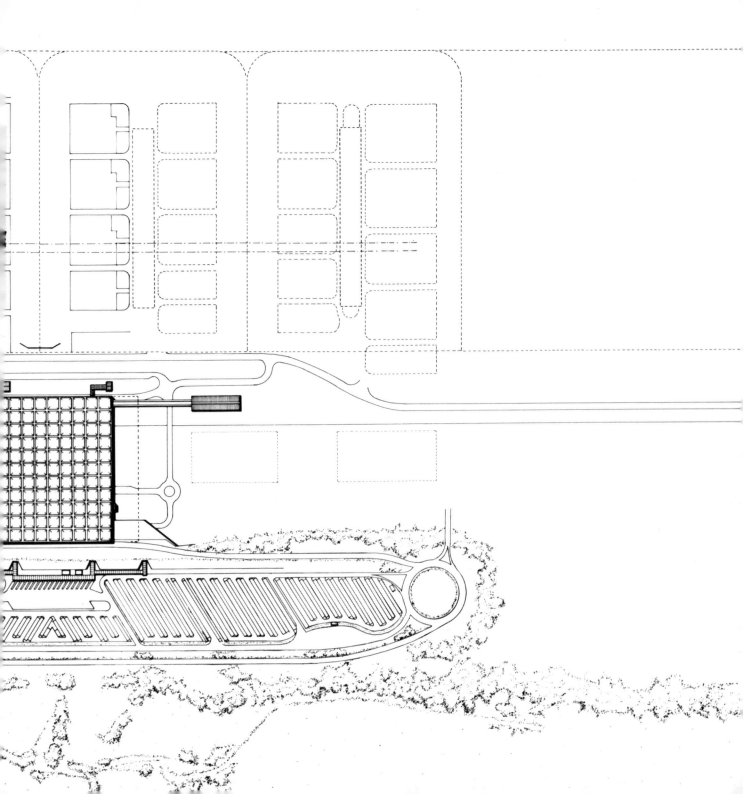

**Plan: concourse level**

**1** Departures concourse
**2** Check-in
**3** Security/passport control
**4** Departure lounge
**5** Shopping
**6** Catering
**7** Domestic channel
**8** Arrivals concourse
**9** Baggage reclaim hall
**10** Customs control
**11** Arrivals concourse
**12** Management offices
**13** Forecourt: coach/taxi drop-off with
British rail station under
**14** Track transit platforms to satellite
**15** Airside coach stations
**16** Track transit system
**17** Short term car park and coach station

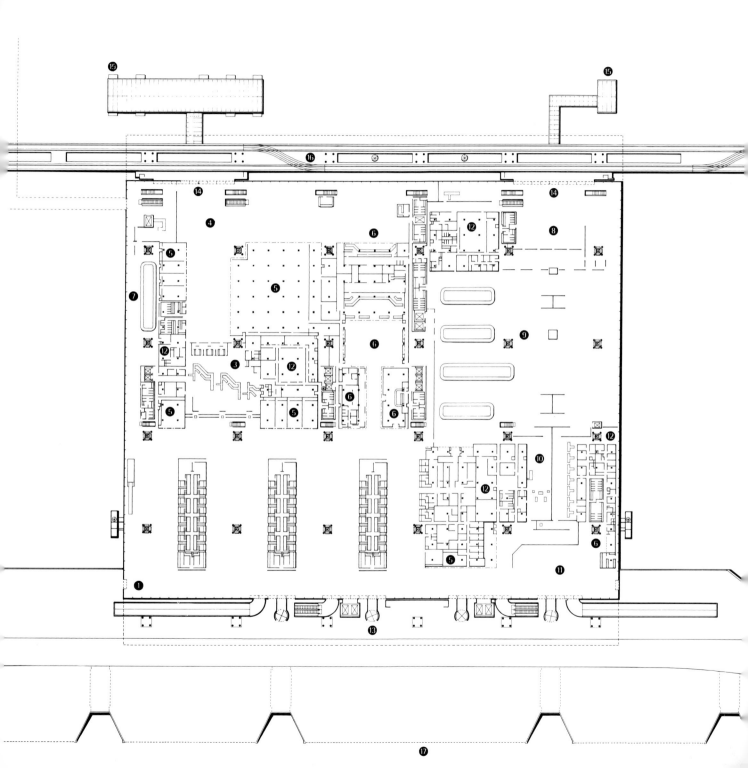

**Plan: undercroft**

**1** Baggage handling (arrivals) hall
**2** Baggage handling (departures) hall
**3** Airside airport operations offices
**4** Duty free customs and general storage
and staff restaurant
**5** Service road
**6** Plant hall
**7** Fresh air supply duct
**8** British rail station
**9** Airside bus stations

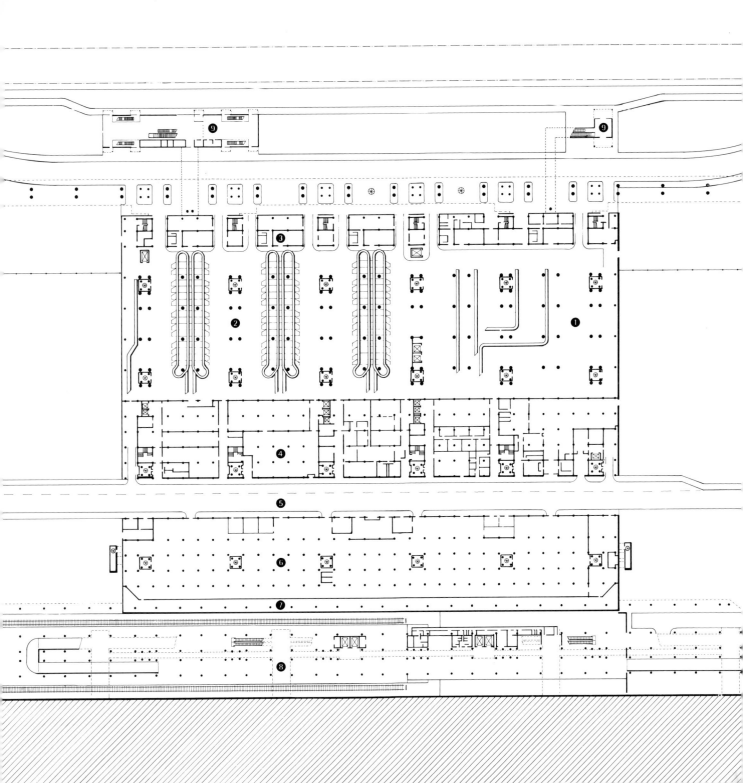

**East-West section**

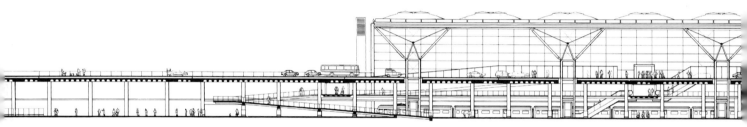

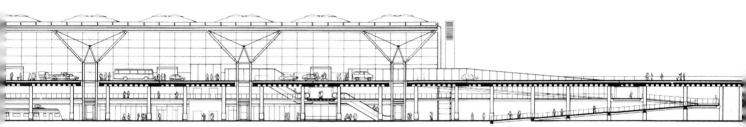

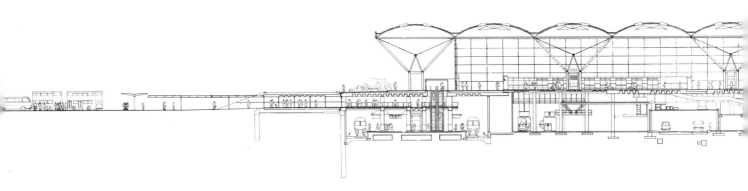

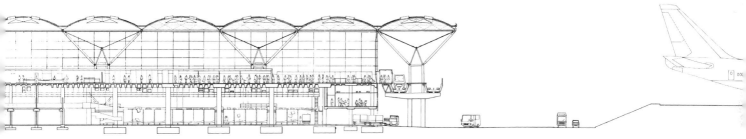

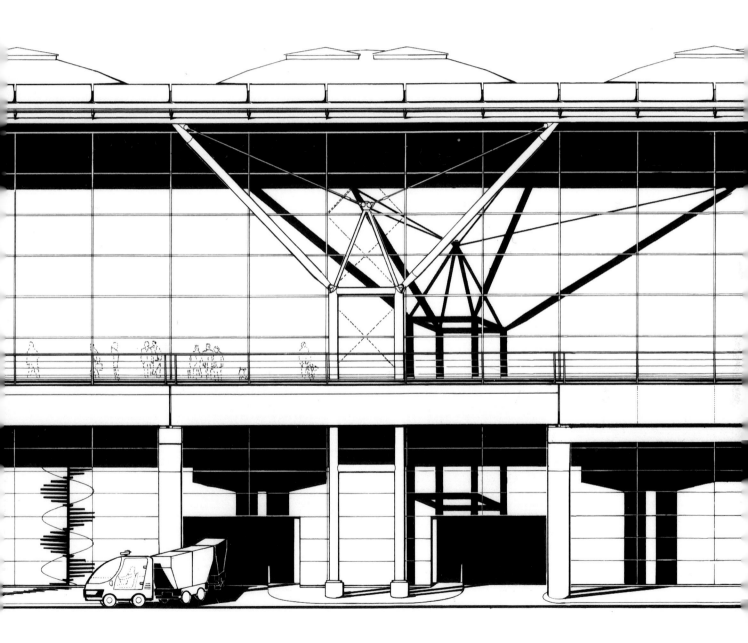

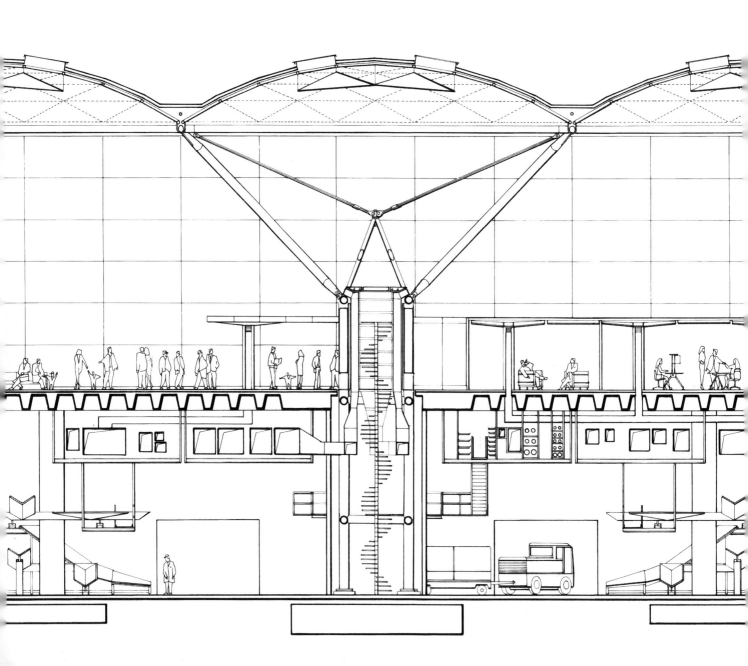

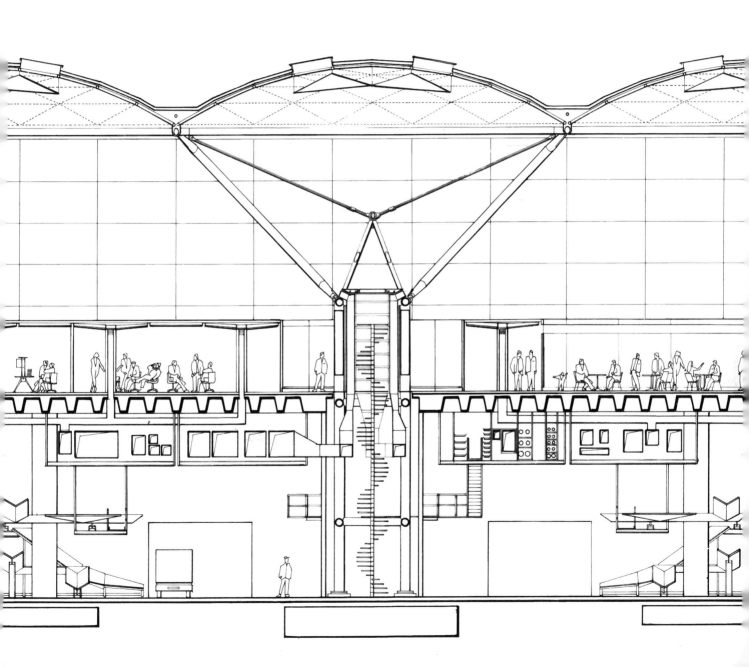

# 104

**Satellite plan: concourse level**

1 Seating area
2 Commercial area
3 Toilets
4 Departures desks
5 Escalators from apron level
6 Desk services

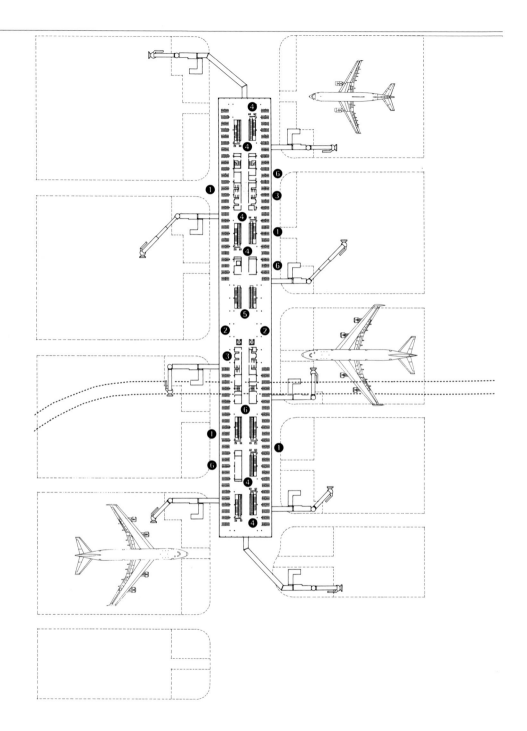

**Satellite plan: arrivals level**

1 Arrivals corridor
2 Departure escalators
3 Link bridges
4 Toilets
5 Ancillary accommodation
6 Escalators from apron level to
concourse level
7 Services

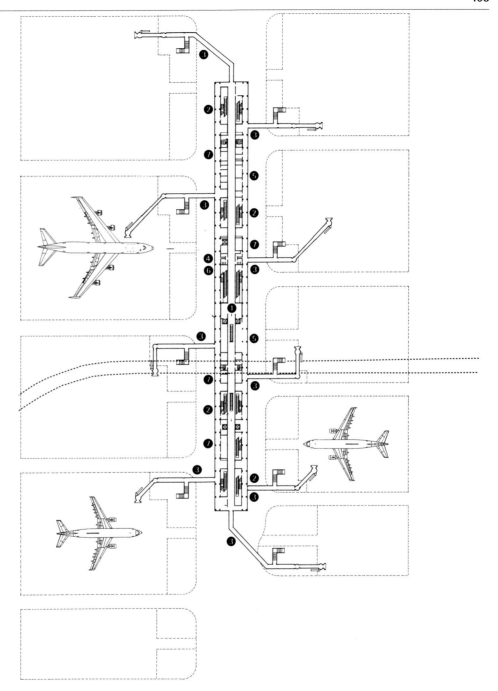

Cross-section through satellite

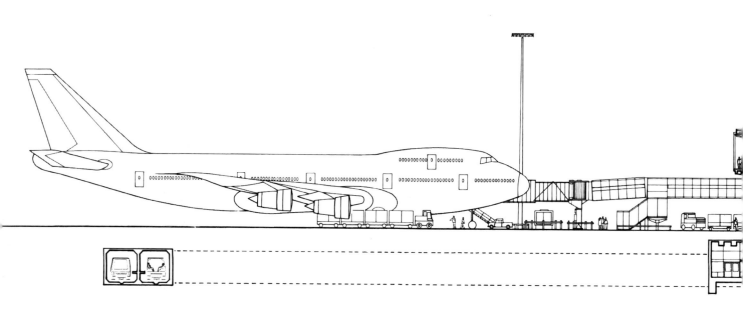

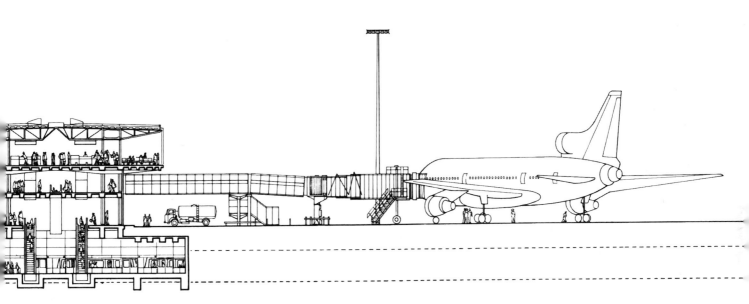

**Variable add-on elements for the
face of the service pods**

1 Directional signs, staff telephone
and hosereel
2 Clock, magazine dispenser
3 Map, information leaflets,
courtesy phone
4 Pod chassis
5 Electrical cupboards
6 Small power
7 Hosereel
8 Fire alarm unit
9 Staff telephone
10 Pull-out information monitors
11 Public address speakers
12 CCTV camera
13 Emergency lights
14 Pod cladding
15 Air supply diffuser
16 Maintenance spiral stair
17 Air return
18 Concourse uplights
19 Roof structure

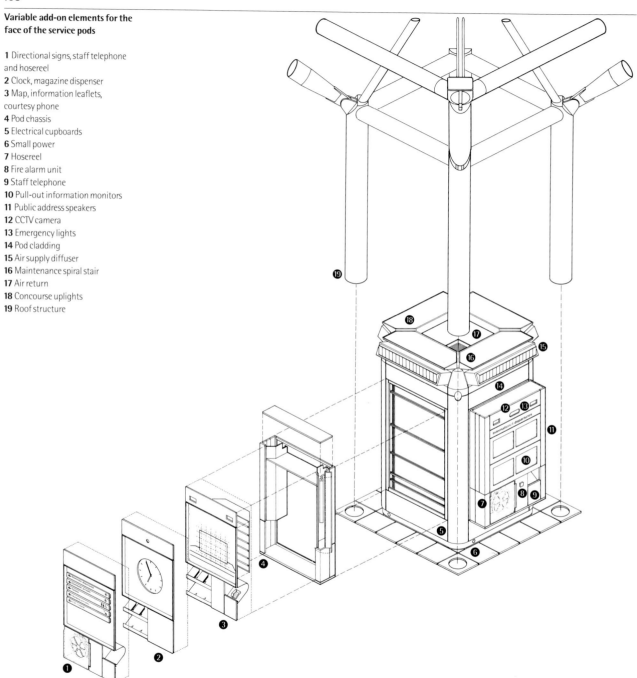

The "tree"

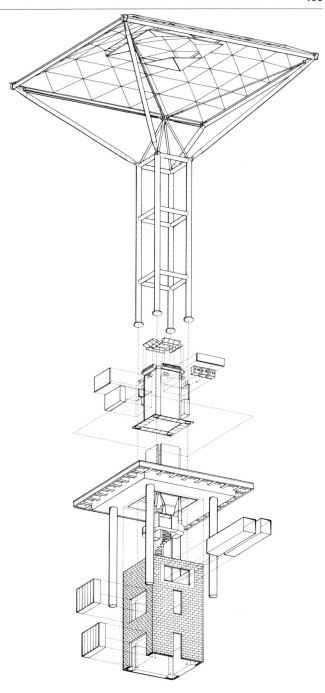

The flexible lighting and ceiling
system for the retail cabins

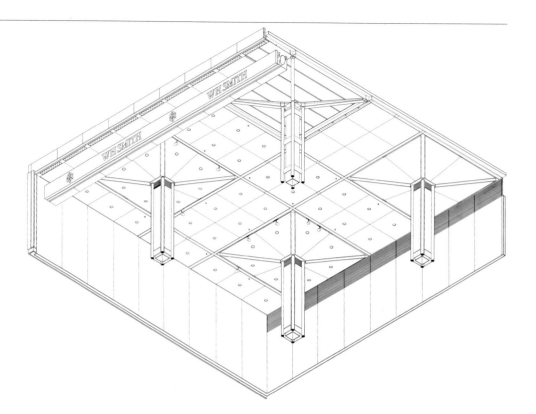

# Chronology of
# Stansted Airport's
# Development

**1943** The main runway laid at
Stansted for the USAF 344 Medium
Bombardment Group

**1946** Stansted first used for civil flights

**1966** The British Airports Authority
(later BAA) begin their association
with Stansted

**1967** A government white paper
proposes that the new London airport
be sited at Stansted

**1969** First Stansted terminal
building finished

**1979** Full inquiry set up to
study further development
of Stansted Airport

**1981** Fosters Associates commissioned
by British Airports Authority to carry
out architectural and planning
feasibility study for new terminal
zone at Stansted

**1985** Government approves BAA
planning application for Stansted
development

**15 March 1991** Her Majesty the Queen
opens the new Stansted
Airport Terminal

# Stansted Airport
# Terminal Zone
# Credits

**The Team**

Client: Stansted Airport Limited

Lead Designer (Terminal and
other Buildings): Foster Associates

Lead Designer (Transit System):
BAA Consultancy

Lead Designer (Infrastructure):
BAA Consultancy

Project Management
Stansted Development Team

**Consultants**

Architecture and Interior Design:
Foster Associates

Structural Engineering (Terminal and
BR Station): Ove Arup & Partners

Structural Engineering (Satellites and
ancillary buildings): BAA Consultancy

Environmental Services Engineering:
BAA Consultancy

Quantity Surveying: BAA with
Beard Dove and Currie & Brown

Construction Management:
Laing Management Ltd and
BAA Consultancy

Movement Systems Engineering:
BAA Consultancy

Lighting (Public Areas):
Claude and Danielle Engle

Acoustics: ISVR Consultancy